Foreword

CABE knows that people value great local parks, streets and green spaces. While providing these facilities had always fallen to the local council, the tide is now changing to let community groups demand and deliver improvements to public space themselves. It is an exciting prospect, though one not without its own difficulties. The enthusiasm, commitment and local knowledge within a community is invaluable but can be hindered by unfamiliar, and sometimes confusing processes and practices to improve a public space. CABE would like to help community groups improve local outdoor spaces. But we do not have the resources to help each group individually. That is why we have written this guide.

John Sorrell CBE
Chair, CABE

The government is committed to empowering and enabling communities everywhere to help shape decisions about the things that matter to them. I welcome the community client guide. It provides valuable practical advice and support for communities so that they can lead improvements to public spaces - a practical opportunity for people to get involved in decisions which affect them and their locality.

So much can be achieved if communities are empowered to get involved in the planning, design, management and maintenance of public spaces, and this is critical if we are to create spaces that communities love, now and in the future.

Baroness Andrews OBE
Communities and Local Government

3

Contents

1 Introduction

Improving public spaces

'We will encourage people of all ages – including children, young people and retired people – to play an active role in deciding what our parks and public spaces should be like and how they should be looked after.'

CABE Space, *Manifesto*, 2004

'We believe that by action at the neighbourhood level, people everywhere can make a significant difference to the quality of our country's public services. In this way, local people can play their part in creating sustainable communities where it is good to live and work.'

Office of the Deputy Prime Minister (ODPM), *Citizen engagement and public services: why neighbourhoods matter*, 2005

All over the country, community groups are becoming involved in improving outdoor spaces. Over the past few years, a range of grants and funding programmes have been made available for this purpose. With the help of the Big Lottery Fund and other funding bodies this looks set to continue. The government is keen for community groups to have greater control over how the local environment is managed and improved. It has set out clear agendas on these issues to make open spaces cleaner, safer and greener. Politicians also recognise that people enjoy great parks and green spaces. The majority of people - 91 per cent - believe that outdoor spaces improve people's quality of life.[1] So, if you have ever thought, 'I could do something great with that space', now could be the time to do it.

© Graeme Mullett

1 CABE, *Public attitudes to architecture and public space: transforming neighbourhoods*, 2005

Types of public space

2 Department for communities and local government, *Planning policy guidance note 17: open space, sport and recreation*, 2002

3 CABE Space, *Green space strategies: a good practice guide*, 2004

This guide is applicable to a range of public space projects ranging from minor improvements to refurbishing existing spaces and creating new ones. Public space is the green spaces, parks, streets, civic squares and other outdoor spaces that are freely accessible to the public and usually free of charge. A useful reference point is the government's *Planning policy guidance note 17*[2] or PPG17. It requires local councils to set local standards for open space and defines outdoor spaces as:

- parks and public gardens
- natural and semi-natural spaces (including wastelands and derelict open land)
- green corridors
- outdoor sports facilities
- amenity green spaces
- provision for children and young people
- allotments, community gardens and city farms
- cemeteries, churchyards and other burial grounds
- accessible countryside in urban fringe areas
- civic spaces, including civic and market squares and other hard surfaced areas designed for pedestrians.

For a project to be successful it is important to know how people move between other spaces, especially children and young people, who are dependent on safe and accessible routes for their ability to play outdoors.

Every space is part of a whole network of different types of outdoor spaces linked by streets, cycleways, canals and alleyways. The local council may have a green or open space strategy that sets out a long-term approach to planning and managing all the spaces in the area. It is useful to get hold of this and understand how the project fits into the strategy and what standards the council has set for achieving quality.[3] Many councils will also have a play strategy which sets out aspirations and needs for play space within an area.

PARKS + GARDENS ①

CEMETERIES + CHURCHYARDS ②

ACCESSIBLE COUNTRYSIDE ③

AMENITY SPACES ④

ALLOTMENTS + GARDENS ⑤

OUTDOOR SPORTS ⑥

GREEN CORRIDORS ⑦

CIVIC SPACES ⑧

CHILD + YOUTH PROVISION ⑨

NATURAL/ SEMI-NATURAL ⑩

Public spaces and design quality

© Michael Harding

There are too many playgrounds that children never use, as they simply aren't in the right place

'Too often, the people who design and construct buildings and parks don't worry about whether they will work properly or what they will cost to run. But the public has to live with badly built, poorly designed buildings and spaces; and taxpayers often have to foot the bill for putting them right again.'

CABE, *The cost of bad design*, 2006

Good design is about creating a place that functions well, both now and in the future. It should also be attractive, providing an inspirational and special place for people. If not designed well, poorly defined places will be created that may cause conflict between different activities and users such as elderly and young people. If spaces lack character and identity people will not want to use them. If they cannot see in and out of a public space people will use it less and crime and anti-social behaviour may creep in.

A public space is continuously changing; planting matures and changes over time and a park in winter will feel very different to one in the summer. The way a place is managed and maintained can have a great impact on how it looks and feels. A well-designed public space will also need to be well-managed.

The Green Flag Award scheme is the national standard for parks and green spaces and its criteria reflect essential factors of a well-maintained space. The aspiration should be to win the award but it is also useful as a checklist for good design and management. Parks and open spaces are judged against the following criteria:

- a welcoming place
- healthy, safe and secure
- clean and well maintained
- sustainability
- conservation and heritage
- community involvement
- marketing
- management.

See www.greenflagaward.org.uk

What is a well-designed public space?

Every public space has different uses and means different things to different people. A well-designed public space meets the needs of all the people using it without favouring one particular group of people. It is flexible enough to meet different needs now and in the future.

A well-designed place has the following qualities:

- sustainability
- character and distinctiveness
- definition and enclosure
- connectivity and accessibility
- legibility
- adaptability and robustness
- inclusiveness
- biodiversity.

See *Glossary* for further explanation of these terms. Adapted from DETR, *By design, urban design in the planning system: towards better practice*, 1999

A good client will think about making outdoor spaces inclusive from the start. The Disability Discrimination Act 1995 (c.50) places a duty on providers of services to take reasonable steps to overcome any difficulties that they may place on disabled people to make use of their service or physical features in their care. It is important that the client is familiar with whatever these reasonable steps might be.
See www.opsi.gov.uk

Mint Street Park Proposal

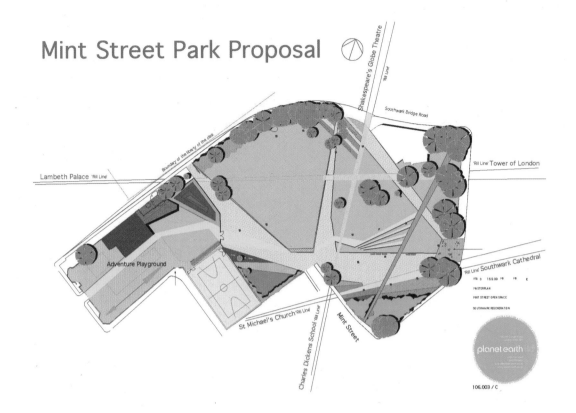

Lambeth Palace 'Rill Line'

Boundary of the liberty of the clink

Shakespeare's Globe Theatre

'Rill Line'

Southwark Bridge Road

'Rill Line' Tower of London

Adventure Playground

St Michael's Church 'Rill Line'

Charles Dickens School 'Rill Line'

Mint Street

'Rill Line' Southwark Cathedral

NB 0 16 9.99 HB   C

MASTERPLAN

MINT STREET OPEN SPACE

SOUTHWARK REGENERATION

planet earth

106.003 / C

In tandem with community needs and ideas, a design was developed to root Mint Street Park within its physical and historical context. It opened up new routes from the surrounding areas so that ancient street patterns that once existed on the site could be renewed and knitted back into the dense urban fabric of the locality

Tackling anti-social behaviour through good design

'A major objective of the Victorians' creation of many new public parks was to create opportunities for improving public behaviour. Their design principles often included laying out serpentine paths and terraces, which created opportunities for people to observe one another, thus discouraging bad behaviour.'

CABE Space, *Decent parks? Decent behaviour? The link between the quality of parks and user behaviour*, 2005

Many communities want to improve spaces because they have been neglected and suffered problems, such as graffiti and vandalism. Investing in good design and good management will be far more effective in tackling these problems than trying to fortify the existing environment. CABE Space's report *Decent parks? Decent behaviour? The link between the quality of parks and user behaviour* provides evidence on how this can be achieved. See www.cabe.org.uk/publications.aspx

Some sites will benefit as much from removal or simplification of features as they will from new elements. It may be that incremental design has changed the site's original purpose. Issues like safety, dealt with in isolation, may have over ridden the original design and well-meaning efforts have put up obstacles and barriers to movement. The project may need to consider opening up vistas and sightlines in parks, even if it includes removing some vegetation to restore a previously well-designed public space to its original design and make people want to use it again.

What is a community client?

A good client is absolutely critical to making a great public space. As well as providing overall leadership and vision, the client is responsible for commissioning designers and contractors, making sure they deliver work to satisfaction. There are many types of community client with differing levels of experience and skills. For the purpose of this guide the client is a community group with little or no experience of managing a public space project. Anyone managing a public space project will need to employ a professional designer and in some cases specialist consultants to help deliver their project. Community clients in particular may need to seek professional advice at an early stage, such as when developing the brief. A community client will almost always benefit from working in partnership with a range of relevant local organisations.

Four key stages of a project

There are four key stages to a public space project: prepare, design, construct and use. Although *Use* focuses on management and maintenance, it is important to consider this at the start of the project to make a space that will be well cared for. Be prepared for the long haul. Projects can take significant time to complete - from one year to five years or more. If this sounds daunting, the examples in this guide show how satisfaction in the process and product far outweighs the time taken and the hard work of the people involved.

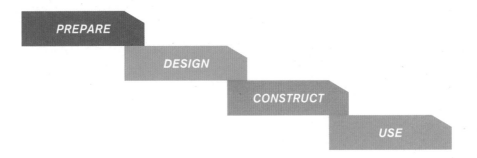

How to use this guide

This guide outlines typical stages in a project but every project is different. A client will need to seek professional advice as necessary to develop their individual project. Dip into this guide for an overview of a client's main roles and responsibilities at each stage. The key questions at the end of each section are prompts to ensure that careful thought has been given to each stage of the project. Use the case studies as inspiration and to learn from the messages they contain, both positive and negative.

Establish the client team and roles

'If we want the very best design, we have to understand a little bit about what we can ask from our professionals. In other words we need to become better clients.'

Neilston community newsletter, *The Space*, November 2005

Rather than one individual, the client for the project is likely to be a team of people with a mix of relevant skills and expertise. Community clients wishing for a greater chance of success should consider setting up a sub-group of an existing body of people that already work well together, such as a tenants' and residents' association. This may bring added benefits, such as an established working relationship with the local council. If the group is already a registered charity, this will bring financial benefits. In setting up a new community group, it is important to decide on the status of the group.

The group may wish to become constituted as an un-incorporated company, which has a written contract such as a constitution to set out the group structure and aims. Alternatively, the group can form an incorporated company or a trust, a more formal structure for groups that want to employ people and own land.[4]

To register a company, trust or registered charity see *Contacts* for details of the Charity Commission and Companies House.

Once the client team is established, everyone should agree to:

- respect strong leadership
- encourage and enthuse team members
- help keep the project on track – managing the budget, monitoring time and quality
- sign off key stages of the project
- stick by the group decisions and not change its mind
- hold only essential meetings – efficiently chaired and minuted
- be generous with praise
- avoid too much jargon
- criticise constructively, in private
- feed back progress to the community
- always keep the big picture in view.

Adapted from CABE, *Creating successful masterplans*, 2004

4 Penn Associates and Countryside Agency, *Making Space, a manual for community groups that manage green space*, 2004

© CMS Design Associates

There was already a strong residents' association at Mapesbury in Brent, London. The client team was established as a sub-group of the residents' association. Suitable skills were drawn from the residents to make up the team, including finance, negotiation, legal expertise, design, public relations, report writing, public spiritedness and general good sense

Typical roles

Project leader
Ensures continued involvement and assistance from other bodies. Needs to have vision and be able to make good decisions when needed; keep everyone enthusiastic and work closely with professionals and specialists. Will chair the client team meetings and achieve consensus.

Project manager
Brings information together, makes day-to-day decisions, monitors progress, controls the budget and is responsible for checking the detail of the project. Usually separate from the project leader and if so, the respective roles should be clarified so that everyone understands them.

Steering group
Includes organisations with specialist skills and representatives of other stakeholders that could include local businesses, specialist organisations and other officers of the local council.

Design champion
Understands design and can help the group to know whether a good design is being proposed. They should not be the same as the design consultant contracted to deliver the project, in order to retain an independent view. This is appropriate for larger projects.

Establish a partnership

Working in partnership with local organisations is essential to creating a successful project. Who is involved in the partnership will depend on the type of project and site. The partnership may be set up as an informal advisory body or be a more formal steering group that is responsible for major decisions. In either case, the partnership should include all land owning and managing representatives as well as any representatives of specialist or local interest groups relevant to the project.

Talk to the local council

It is advisable to talk to the local council before starting the project. Roles within local councils depend on many circumstances. A district or borough council is more likely to have responsibility for maintaining parks and green spaces than a county council and a parish council may own a large amount of public space. Potential sources of advice and examples of support to expect include:

- elected councillors, who can raise the profile of the project
- planning officers, who can help test the viability of the project and advise on planning regulations and site ownership
- parks and green space officers, who may have a strategy to identify priorities and can advise on management and maintenance
- street care and cleansing officers, who may provide on-site staff and advise of the impact of the project on litter collection and rubbish collection services
- the local strategic partnership, which can provide a route for the project to gain funding and recognition
- youth and community officers, who can involve young people in the project
- ecology officers, who can help identify the animals and plants already on a site and help encourage biodiversity.

'Brent Parks Service's policy is to promote a range of partnerships to improve and develop spaces, evolving different models to suit local conditions and enthusiasms. Mapesbury Dell is an example of a close working partnership with a residential community.'

Shaun Faulkner, Brent Parks Service

© Graeme Mullett

Brent's Community Parks Warden service has been introduced to help keep the parks tidy and safe and to provide a friendly welcome to the parks

Involve other partners and roles

Other partners in a public space project may include voluntary sector organisations such as Groundwork Trusts, Wildlife Trusts or Civic Trusts. They may advise on specialist areas such as the value of wildlife or help raise additional funding. Ideally, the same representative should stay involved throughout the project. Funders may also wish to be partners. For more ideas see *Further information*.

Identify, consult and involve people

Identify stakeholders

The client is responsible for identifying how to involve local people in the project. This may include early consultation to shape the brief as well as asking local people for their opinions on proposed designs. The client is unlikely to be representative of everyone in the area, and needs to be prepared to take the views of many other people into consideration. It is now generally accepted that involving people in design and care of public space is necessary for long-term success of a project. Local people can provide useful information and the project can, in return, help to increase their skills and confidence. It will also result in a public space that will be popular.

Benefits provided by a well-used public space:

- creates natural surveillance
- makes a place welcoming
- ensures a sense of safety.

'Ownership is key to successful public spaces whether green open space or town centre squares. This requires input and action planning at grass roots level. Equally, there needs to be an exchange of skills – the community has not only ideas, but tacit knowledge of places that can and do reveal extraordinary things.'

Steve McAdam, Fluid

Doorstep Greens © Natural England

Photos of students' work on display for members of the Dukes Meadows Trust

Consulting people on their views as a one-off exercise will result in far fewer benefits than involving people in an ongoing process of participation. There are many organisations that support community activity and these may bring valuable resources into the project.

Some or all of the following people should be on board and the nature of the project will determine their roles:

– landowner
– local council departments
– funders (short-term)
– services such as the police and fire services
– local residents' bodies
– local businesses and any other long-term investors
– amenity groups
– voluntary sector, for example youth clubs and housing associations
– local people that don't belong to amenity groups and residents' bodies
– local politicians: elected council members, parish and town councillors
– young people, as future users and custodians
– access groups/access officer
– visitors to the area.

This list includes those with a financial or legal interest in the project as well as current and future users. Take time to listen to any concerns they may have. In this way, what is created will serve the needs of everyone. Professionals and national guidance may be helpful in demonstrating experience beyond that of the client and so allay fears others may have, especially about potential misuse of the space. CABE offers guidance about design, management and maintenance issues, that can be downloaded for free www.cabe.org.uk

Drawing up a consultation plan at the outset will help decide who to involve and how to involve them. The plan should be flexible enough to adapt to any issues that may arise. In developing a consultation plan, consider the following questions:

- why is the consultation being carried out?
- who should be involved and what interest will they have in the project?
- what previous consultation has been carried out that may provide a useful starting point?
- what existing groups are in the area that may have an interest?
- what kind of information or outcomes do you want to get out of the consultation?
- at what stage will it be important to involve different groups of people?
- what kind of techniques will achieve the desired outcomes?

There are a number of tried and tested consultation techniques such as questionnaires and doorstep interviews, that may need to be carried out. Design consultants with experience of working with communities should be able to advise on suitable approaches to consultation. One of the main challenges will be to engage all sectors of the community, including those who don't currently use the site. There may be barriers that only they perceive.

Different types of community

'Working with a community you inevitably become exposed to all the internal tensions that exist in any community – the idea of a community having a single voice or viewpoint is a myth.'

Ben Hamilton-Baillie, Hamilton-Baillie Associates

The community itself may be difficult to define. The client should take time to learn about the demographics of the area and also the services that are provided to support different people in the community: older people, people with disabilities, faith and ethnic groups, refugees and asylum seekers to make sure the project accommodates the needs of all the different people in the area.

Groundwork UK has identified several types of community that are:

- Territorial - individuals brought together by a common locality, such as the same street or district serving their neighbourhood
- Interest - people brought together by a common interest or occupation, for example, an environmental group, friends group or Neighbourhood Watch
- Identity - defined by a shared feeling of identity, such as religious and ethnic groups.

Groundwork UK, *Working with communities a toolkit*, 2002

Involving young people

It is essential to involve young people in the project for it to be a long-term success, as they are its custodians of the future. Young people can play a valuable part in the design and after-care of the project, as well as learning skills from respecting others to caring for plants. There may also be special pots of funding to support their involvement.

Young people have strong views and may not understand the boundaries of what is possible. However, they can bring creativity and fresh ideas to the project. Get in touch with local Sure Start and Connexions advisors, youth and play workers, school learning mentors and school councils, who can all bring young people into the project. Given the right conditions – meet them at times and in places they feel comfortable with – young people instinctively consider the needs of younger children and older people in design and can help to identify potential opportunities for misuse.[5]

© Kinnear Landscape Architects

5 CABE Space, *What would you do with this space? Involving young people in the design and care of urban spaces*, 2004

Kinnear Landscape Architects with Sheffield Wildlife Trust met with the local primary school and gave a brief introduction, describing what a landscape architect does and showed ideas for the park. All the young people stated they would like to help build the park and could plant trees and wildflowers

Understand the site

Find the right site

Communities often get involved in projects because they want to improve their local park or create new facilities in their local area. If the project is focused on a particular site, the client team must identify the right range of facilities to be provided. However if the project is about creating much needed facilities in an area, the challenge is to find the most appropriate place to site them. Check if the local council has identified public spaces that would benefit from improvement. By improving public space, the project is helping the council fulfill its duties to its residents. There may also be a masterplan for the area that has identified public space for improvement. By tying into an existing regeneration project, the group may gain access to funding and resources. Above all, it is very important to identify the need for the project.

Secure the landowner's permission

If the land is in the ownership of the local council its agreement to the project is needed. If it is uncertain who owns the land, which is often the case, the UK Land Registry may be able to provide this information. It is then essential to get the landowner's written permission for the client team to work on the site, as well as to understand everyone's respective responsibilities. See www.landreg.gov.uk

Establish what restrictions apply

The client needs to check with the local council's planning department whether there are any planning designations that may restrict its use of the site or if permission is required to implement its plans. There may be, for example, special designations protecting the site for its nature conservation value. The client also needs to establish with the landowner what it can do with the site in the future and what level of ownership or management arrangement is possible. A long lease gives a good level of control, while a freehold isn't always achievable.

Mick McGrath, Big Lottery Fund's Head of
Region (East Midlands) and Carolyn Robson,
Rushley Mead School, Head Teacher with
£50,000 cheque awarded by BIG for the
Leicester school's project to make playing
fields safer and more accessible

Secure funding

© Heritage Lottery Fund

Most public space projects are funded from more than one source. It can take a long time to gather enough funding for a project. However, funders' timescales also mean that the client still needs to deliver parts of the project to tight deadlines. This guide does not provide detailed advice about funding, nevertheless, a few useful signposts are provided. National funding streams that fund public space projects include the Big Lottery Fund and the Heritage Lottery Fund, for more details see *Further information*.

The charity GreenSpace organises conferences on sourcing funding for parks and green spaces and has a community network of groups that share their own experiences on this and many other issues. A useful publication is GreenSpace, *Claiming your share*, 2003. See www.green-space.org.uk

The local council may be able to contribute some funding to the project. To make the case for funding the client will need to demonstrate how the project will deliver the council's aims. Obtain and reference the community strategy, biodiversity action plan or a green or open space strategy, which may be found on the council's website.

A useful statistic for making strong funding bids is the level of deprivation in the area – this is listed in the Index of Multiple Deprivation (IMD). It consists of a ward level index prepared by government made up of six indicators including levels of education and skills, employment levels and income. See www.statistics.gov.uk

Appoint the design consultant

At the outset the community client needs to understand the relationship between size and complexity of project, and type of consultant needed. They will need a lead design consultant but may need to supplement with others with particular expertise, such as surveyors or structural engineers. Consider consultants carefully as they are a considerable component of project costs and the client will need to manage them carefully and effectively.

Choose the right design skills

It is important to decide the appropriate design skills for the project. These are summarised in the box *Types of design professionals*. A landscape architect is likely to be the most appropriate design professional for a public space project. This guide only summarises the key steps to appointing a design consultant, however it signposts useful resources. These include a series of guides published by the Landscape Institute - the professional body for landscape architects, which the client should purchase and take time to read carefully. The guides are:

Doorstep Greens © Natural England

– Appointing a chartered landscape architect, guidelines for best value
– Engaging a landscape consultant, guidance for clients on fees
– Guide to procedure for competitive tendering
– The landscape consultant's appointment.

See www.landscapeinstitute.org

Types of design professional

Landscape architects sometimes known as landscape designers, use their design expertise and technical skills to improve the environment in a variety of external settings - both urban and rural. With a range of relevant skills, from planting design to hard construction detailing, landscape architects can lead a project from conception to completion on site. They will also will be able to advise on management planning. To find the right landscape architect for the job, contact the Landscape Institute, which has a list of chartered landscape architects www.landscapeinstitute.org

Architects design and construct new buildings, restore and conserve old ones, and the spaces around them. They can also oversee the construction process. To find a suitable architect for the job, contact the Royal Institute of British Architects (RIBA) www.riba.org.uk

Public artists can add richness and the unexpected to a project. They may interpret the existing site and area, drawing on local features, history and character in their artworks. Public art often works best when integrated into a project from the outset and public artists may work alongside other consultants very effectively. Take advice from local arts councils, www.artscouncil.org.uk and architecture centres www.architecturecentres.net

Quantity surveyors calculate the costs of a project before and during construction. They study plans drawn up by a landscape architect and calculate the types and quantities of materials required, and the cost of time and labour. The results are itemised into a 'bill of quantities' which building contractors use as a basis for estimating costs www.rics.org

Land surveyors measure, define and illustrate, either digitally or graphically in the form of maps or plans, the physical features of a site's surface. To find a suitable surveyor, contact the Royal Institution of Chartered Surveyors www.rics.org

Structural engineers are involved in the design and supervision of the construction of structures such as pavilions and sports facilities. Their specialist skills ensure the structure has the strength required to perform its function safely, economically and with a shape and appearance that is visually satisfying. For more information contact the Institution of Structural Engineers www.istructe.org.uk

There is a variety of ways to appoint a design consultant. Partners with experience of project management such as the local council or a Groundwork Trust may be able to help select a suitable design consultant with the right skills for the project. They may also help guide the client on the process of appointing the consultant. In addition, the main funder may wish to approve this process. If the client decides on a formal tendering process, standard procedures include setting a common deadline for submissions, opening tenders at the same time and assessing suitability against the same criteria.

Make sure at the end of the process to record the client team's approval and issue a contract. For smaller projects it is possible to appoint a consultant by letter, however, for larger projects there are standard forms of appointment. Note that a separate contract will be required for each consultant chosen. These can be found on the websites for each profession. It is important to provide feedback on performance to all the tenderers not appointed.

Create a positive working relationship

The client will work closely with the design consultant, and so needs to be able to form a positive working relationship with them. The clearer the client is in terms of what it wants from the project, the easier it will be for the consultant to deliver it. Remember, this is a creative process and it is unlikely that it will be all plain sailing.

© Groundwork UK

**How to appoint
a landscape architect**

Direct appointment
Select a landscape architect who has appropriate experience for the project. Discuss the project and establish what their fees might be. This will provide a mutual understanding of what is required through a process of negotiation.

Competitive fee tendering
The client must specify the project and services required exactly so that all tenderers price the same work. A written and agreed brief will be required and this process will require sufficient time to produce all the detailed information needed. Many funders will require competitive selection of consultants to ensure value for money but the process may not be cost effective for small or phased projects.

Design competitions
Hold a design competition to bring fresh ideas to the project.
There are different ways of organising competitions and expert advice should be sought on the best approach. The Landscape Institute and Royal Institute of British Architects can advise. Unless the purpose of the competition is to generate lots of new ideas for the site, a detailed brief will be required to ensure submissions deliver what the client team is looking for.

The Landscape Institute's guide sets out the recommended processes in detail see the Landscape Institute, *Appointing a chartered landscape architect: guidelines for best value*, 2000.

Develop a vision for the site

© Camlin Lonsdale

'On completion, the West Bromwich Town Square will provide a valuable recreational resource in the form of high quality public realm not found in the town centre at present. We want our design team to help us make a place that many will come to value and which, through time, will begin to gather a cherished collective memory.'

Vision for West Bromwich Town Square as stated in Sandwell Metropolitan Borough Council, *West Bromwich Town Square consultants' brief for design services*, 2004

'A vision helps shape what happens on the site, giving it coherence and a real sense of identity and place. A vision is likely to derive from an understanding of the characteristics of a site, its history and geography, to suggest how a sense of place can be created and related to what is there already. It is important that the vision is not lost during the development of the design, so as it develops, the plan must be constantly checked against the original vision.'

CABE, *Creating successful masterplans: a guide for clients*, 2004

The vision is usually a written statement setting out the shared aspirations for the project. It is also useful to include images and diagrams.
An initial vision can be developed early in the project by the client and key stakeholders. This can be done by holding a visioning workshop with stakeholders to decide on a vision that everyone can keep in their minds; it can also help to manage their expectations. The client may need to adapt this later on to take on board views of the wider community.

Many successful projects started with the client and stakeholders visiting other places and bringing back design ideas. Bear in mind that the grand designs in other places may need to be adapted to reflect the needs of the local context.

© The Glass-House Community Led Design

See your public space in a new light after training

Training is invaluable for community groups involved in local regeneration schemes. It enables them to be empowered, confident that what they are doing is right and professional when executing their projects – important when it is public money they are spending.

The Glass-House Community Led Design offers a suite of highly subsidised residential training courses. The courses aim to give community groups the skills, knowledge and confidence to take informed positive action in the design of their neighbourhoods and bring about real sustainable change. The courses are run in Chester at Trafford Hall, home of the National Communities Resource Centre.

Spaces by Design, developed and run for The Glass-House Community Led Design by Groundwork Manchester, Salford and Trafford, focuses on the design of public spaces. This course examines the role of public spaces within a community, exploring inspiring real life examples of successful schemes for communal spaces, parks and play areas. Spaces by Design helps participants gain the design skills and confidence necessary to move on from inspiration to action.

Courses are available to tenant, resident and community groups. See www.theglasshouse.org.uk or www.traffordhall.com

Develop the brief

The brief sets the collective aspirations and goals of a project. A range of information is needed to inform the brief such as how people use the space and what they think of it, physical characteristics and history.

A survey is required at the start of any project to identify the physical characteristics of the site. The client can save time and money by providing information about the site, such as whether it has any planning designations which may restrict its use. Unless it is a particularly small site, a land survey will need to be commissioned from a specialist company that will provide information on existing physical features of the space such as:

– dimensions of the site
– different levels across the site
– existing boundaries
– existing structures
– services to the site
– existing trees and vegetation.

It is also useful to identify how the site is used – how people will come and go. Putting some time into initial user surveys and visitor counts will provide invaluable information to the design consultant. As part of this process, consider the future of the space and the wider area. Consider the site in context – look beyond the site boundaries at how it links with the streets and spaces around. This is also the time to consider how the site will be maintained to a high standard on completion. The brief for the project could usefully refer to the criteria of the Green Flag Award scheme, the national standard for parks and green spaces. Its criteria reflect essential factors of a well-maintained space. See www.greenflagaward.org.uk

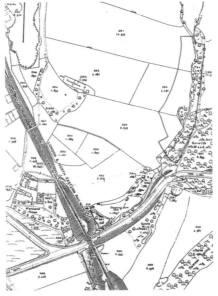

Cookson Park: Opportunities for change. Kinnear Landscape Architects were selected for Cookson Park by the client and community representatives. By analysing the history and context of the site the brief was then developed

1. Current layout
2. The site as it used to be: old field and woodland layout
3. Network of existing green space
4. Making the park green again and reducing areas of hard landscape
5. Views and re-establishing links to Scraith Wood

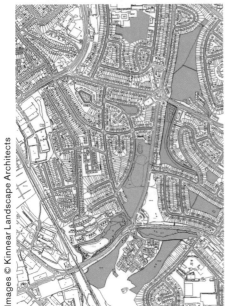

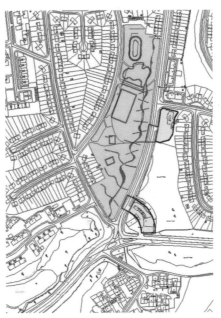

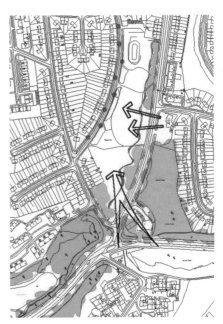

Images © Kinnear Landscape Architects

Prepare the outline brief

An outline brief will be needed on projects where the scope of the project is uncertain and some initial feasibility work is required. It is also useful when a design consultant needs to be appointed to help develop the detailed brief with the client team.

The outline brief will include a selection of key information:

- site description and location
- details of the client team and relevant partners
- all relevant baseline information such as any planning restrictions
- a preliminary vision for the site
- outline timetable for delivering the project
- outline budget and resources available
- provision for maintenance and management.

Prepare the outline budget

Chiswick Farmers Market: the market is organised by Dukes Meadows Trust and the revenue raised from stall holders goes back into projects to upgrade Dukes Meadows

At this stage, the full cost of the project is unknown (it is identified at the detailed design stage). However, it is possible to set an outline budget that will include how much money is available and what it can be spent on, and include other limiting factors such as the timescales of spending different funding. The overall capital costs of projects featured in this guide are useful to note, although each one will have its own individual circumstances. For all but the simplest projects it is recommended that a professional is appointed who will be responsible for cost estimates as designs are developed and controlling costs during construction. This is usually the design consultant, although on larger, more complex projects a quantity surveyor may need to be appointed.

The client needs to consider the project costs from the outset. These include one-off capital costs and ongoing revenue costs:

Capital costs
- materials
- equipment
- construction
- fees for designers and other professionals
- contingency – the part of the budget kept for emergencies.

Revenue costs
- insurance
- people's time including that of the client
- maintenance and on-site staff.

Prepare the outline timetable

It is essential to ensure that on-going maintenance costs are budgeted for. It's very easy for sites to decline in quality as soon as they are handed over for maintenance. Every project will have different requirements and the timetable needs to be tailored as necessary, but use the information provided in the relevant sections of this guide to set out a draft project timetable. For example, whereas a sketch design may take about a month for the designer to prepare, the detailed design may take six months and the whole project up to five years. Due to the nature of many funding streams, it is likely that the project will be completed in stages. Once a design consultant is appointed, they wil be able to help refine the timetable.

Consider a feasibility study

A feasibility study identifies any technical limitations to the project and may be needed for larger or more complex projects. It revises and tests the brief, challenges the timescale and whether the budget is enough. It can be a useful process for scoping what is possible on a site or identifying potential locations for new facilities in an area. People may build expectations around the vision and so feed back any reasons why it could not be achieved. It is helpful to appoint an independent consultant to carry out this study so that significant risk can be identified. The client should be very clear about what to include.

A feasibility study should contain the following information:

- technical: relating to the site possibilities, constraints and likely permissions
- financial: including initial fundraising and long-term cost implications
- organisational: considering the ability of the group to carry out the project and extra skills needed
- programme: the length of time needed.

Adapted from CABE, *Creating excellent buildings*, 2004

Develop a business case

Some funders require a business case which explains the background to the project, why it may change and identifies any business benefits likely to result from it. Examples include generating revenue from a café or running events. Although these will change over the timescale of the project, it is important to include them, stating the cash flow needed and when any benefits will come to fruition, as well as identifying risks.

The business case includes:

– capital costs
– revenue costs
– sources of funds
– any business benefits expected from the project
– comparison with benefits from using funds in a different way
– how viable the proposals are economically.

Adapted from CABE, *Creating excellent buildings*, 2004

Prepare the full brief

'If there is little experience of this in the community, they should seek help from experts. The brief is very important and should act as a quality steering tool in the process. Often projects can be poor as a result of a poor brief.'

Gehl Architects

Once the initial preparation work is complete, including any feasibility work and public consultation, a final detailed brief can be drawn up. This will provide the basis for the final agreement with the design consultant and will guide the course of the project. The full brief describes the intentions of the project, the services needed and on what basis the project or commission will be arranged. It is important that the brief represents the views and aspirations of the wider community and is approved by the client and key stakeholders.

The full brief will include a selection of key information:

– site description and location
– details of the client team and relevant partners
– all relevant baseline information such as any planning restrictions
– vision for the site
– timetable for delivering the project
– budget and resources available
– expected outcomes.

SPACE

Key questions

- Are suitable skills available in the client team?

- Has the client identified and involved local people in developing the project?

- Has the landowner's permission been granted?

- Is the site subject to any planning restrictions?

- Has a professional design consultant been appointed?

- Has a clear vision been agreed?

- Is the project feasible?

- Will the site be maintained to a high standard on completion of the project?

Create a model partnership: London

Client and partners Bankside Open Spaces Trust (BOST),
London Borough of Southwark, local businesses and residents

Designers various

Size 10 sites various locations

Current stage ongoing (10 years since inception)

Cost up to £500,000 each

Engaging the BOST model of a trust, not for a single project but over many, has a number of benefits; it can build and sustain knowledge and skills, relationships can be built over time and it can pool resources.

Dog fouling, litter, vandalism, rough sleeping, drug use and illegal fires were frequent problems in many of south London's parks and open spaces. They became a significant issue when the area underwent intense regeneration and re-development, threatening existing open spaces. So, in 1996, the Bankside Open Spaces Trust (BOST) was established to combat these difficulties. BOST's aim was to foster a sense of community through the protection, care and development of local green spaces.

BOST has become a vehicle for the Bankside community to act as a client and affect the quality of local green space, and it encourages high aspirations. The board of trustees is taken from the residential and business communities and can also draw on a panel of expert advisers. BOST actively keeps everyone informed of project development and activities taking place in its network of green spaces. Helen Firminger, director, explains:

'It is important while giving clear information, not to patronise people but to expect them to be able to grasp the issues in a mature way, as they are frequently able to do. When supporting the progress of a project, it is also

© Bankside Open Spaces Trust

Pupils from adjacent Cathedral and St Joseph's schools provided a display of maypole dancing at the official reopening of Red Cross Garden, marking the culmination of several years work by Bankside Open Spaces Trust

© Bankside Open Spaces Trust

The Red Cross Garden is the first project BOST agreed to maintain fully on completion. To look after the garden, BOST buys in services from the Council, runs a gardening club and sources other services itself

important to let people know what they are in for, by describing the process at the outset.'

With each new project, a steering group is set up and facilitated by BOST, with representation drawn from those living or working nearby. The steering group becomes the forum for key decision-making. BOST also acts as the community client when the London Borough of Southwark leads projects. Typically, consultation identifies people's needs and these are written into a design brief which the steering group reviews and approves. A design team with appropriate skills is appointed and once the design is developed in detail, landscape contractors are then appointed. BOST staff work with the steering group responsible for each project to manage the consultation and compile the brief. BOST remains involved in all its spaces, organising activities and events and contributing to maintaining their condition and sense of security.

Its most recent project, the Red Cross Garden, is the first it has agreed to maintain fully on completion. This will be under a lease from the council. To look after the garden, BOST will buy some services from the council, run a gardening club and source others itself. It will also base staff in the garden.

You need to know

The BOST model of a trust can provide effective feedback to the council through an established channel proven to effect change. It can develop and improve its ability to manage design over time. To be effective in taking on a number of spaces, it helps to set out a definite policy of intention and methods of execution, as well as developing a clear design management strategy. Why not visit Mint Street Park, where Planet Earth landscape architects were awarded the Landscape Institute's Community involvement award in 2004?

See Bankside Open Spaces Trust, *In my backyard, growing a sense of place in Bankside,* 2002 and www.bost.org.uk or visit Mint Street Park, London SE1.

47

Be ambitious about your place: Glasgow

Client and partners Space to Live, with East Renfrewshire Council, Neilston Village Regeneration Group, Architecture and Design Scotland (A+DS)

Designers Gillespies, with Gehl Architects and Hamilton-Baillie Associates

Size various

Current stage A+DS enabling

Cost £32,000 for consultation process from Scottish Community Action Research Fund and Scottish Executive's National Programme on Architecture

Bringing high-level thinking to the Neilston project, and involving the community from the start, has raised aspirations to transform public space to become the heart of community life.

Once a major centre for the cotton industry, Neilston near Glasgow, Scotland, has pockets of severe deprivation and high unemployment. The character of Neilston's townscape has suffered over time, with piecemeal demolition and rebuild. The aim of this project is to transform the village with higher density and high quality development, re-design the roads, streets and paths and see public space as the focus for community life to develop. Pauline Gallacher, volunteer project manager and local resident describes the ambitions of the project:

'New Neilston is a new way of place-making. In this respect, inspirational design and planning will not add value to the project - they are the values of the project.'

The villagers held a public workshop called the Big Do, to begin forming a masterplan for the area, by focusing on public space. They invited international high level thinkers to the event, preceded by evening talks by experts on urban design, to explore spatial options for the village. Residents

Revving up for NEILSTON's BIG DO....

CELEBRITY DESIGNER
TEATIME TALKS

Talk 1 Ben Hamilton Baillie

SHARED SPACE: RECONCILING PEOPLE, PLACES AND TRAFFIC

One of the key problem areas in the village is the relationship between cars and people. *People places* have become *car places* – and more cars mean less space for people. Is it either/or or can cars people and other moving things find a way of living together? Our speaker is an part of the expert team in the European Union project to research and develop shared space. He will have some radical and controversial things to say.

S P A C E T O L I V E
N E I L S T O N

Friday 11 November
Glen Halls (upper)
6 – 7.30pm

Wine and sandwiches provided!

Talk 2 ➡

© Pauline Gallacher

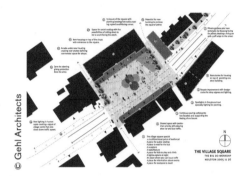

© Gehl Architects

A creative exploration in space by Gehl Architects - raising ambition, posing challenges - first steps in a journey towards an officially commissioned masterplan

You need to know

looked at the village layout and pedestrian networks connecting these spaces and identified five key meeting places or hubs. While everyone was together, they created scenarios on how people across the generations used and perceived spaces. The Big Do was part of a yearlong, unhurried consultation, which aimed to create opportunities for the community to reflect in a critical and informed way about the possibilities for development and change.

The project came to the attention of Architecture and Design Scotland (A+DS) and an offer of enabling was made to the local council, to allow the aspirations of the project to be taken forward. Space to Live (now Neilston Development Trust) is working with a seconded planner and an A+DS enabler under the auspices of Neilston Village Regeneration Group to produce a report proposing the creation of a masterplan owned by both council and community.

This grassroots initiative has drawn in high-profile professional expertise which otherwise would not have been brought to the regeneration process. Bringing high-level thinking to the project, however, has not resulted in imposing grand designs on the community, since it was involved in developing the vision from the start. Even when time is limited, it makes sense to pay attention to managing consultation well. Doing this will contribute to the long-term success of the project.

See the site in development www.neilstonspacetolive.co.uk or visit Neilston, Glasgow G78.

The design process

This guide takes as a first principle that a professional design consultant is essential to ensure a good quality public space is created, and so does not offer guidance on how to design for community clients. However, it is important for the client to communicate and discuss design issues with the consultant to get the best out of the project. This following section highlights some key design issues to consider.

Design issues to consider

Scale
The overall scale of the space is important to get right. Think about large scale places where people will mix and meet each other, as well as smaller, more intimate space for contemplation and relaxation.

Scale: Cresent Gardens, Gosport
Enclosure: Peace Gardens, Sheffield
Circulation: Hulme Park, Manchester

Green Flag Award scheme © Innes Marlow

Enclosure

How the space is defined and divided is a practical issue that will affect the site security. It will also affect how a site feels to be in. It includes the definition of space, through changing the ground level and using vertical elements to create barriers and enclosure around or within the site.

Circulation

How the space is accessed and how people will move through it will help determine its layout. Paths should be laid out in a way that enables people to reach their destination in a logical and efficient manner. The most direct route people will want to take is a desire line. These routes need to be designed into the circulation space of a site to avoid worn routes through areas of grass or planting unless this detracts from the visual integrity of a space.

Materials

The project is likely to consist of hard and soft materials and may include buildings or structures. Materials should be attractive to the eye with good use of shape, colour, texture and form. The soft landscape is the natural elements, such as plant materials and the soil itself. The hard landscape is the elements added to this, such as paving, gravel, walkways, irrigation systems, retaining walls, sculpture, street amenities, fountains, and other mechanical features. When choosing materials consider ease of maintenance, local context and character, overall design objectives, functionality and cost.

Topography and levels

Sites will have various surface features, including natural and man-made features. This is known as the topography and is shown on the site plan as contour lines. The contour lines map connecting points of the same ground level and are used to measure slope and drainage. Few sites are completely flat and changes in ground level across the site can be used to create a variety of experiences from high viewpoints to sunken, enclosed sheltered areas. Changes in level can be dealt with informally and blend in with surrounds or made into a feature.

Bottom © Planet Earth Ltd. Top © J&L Gibbons

Drainage

To prevent pooling of water in unwanted areas, it is important to consider how water will run off from the site's surface or subsurface, such as through sewers or natural means. Sustainable drainage offers numerous environmental and cost benefits. For instance, grassed verges instead of kerb and channeling allow natural drainage along paths and roads.

Left © Nicole Collomb. Right © David Millington/BDP

Lighting

Consider installing lighting around structures or along paths that are used by the public when dark. Well-lit spaces will deter anti-social behaviour and can highlight selected features throughout the space, such as uplighting trees or buildings.

Materials: Edward Square, London
Topography and levels: Mint Street Park, London
Drainage: Malmo, Sweden
Lighting: Cathedral Gardens, Manchester

Once the design consultant has been successfully appointed, the client's main role is to support the design process, provide feedback to the consultant when needed and ensure timely decision-making. The client team must nominate someone, usually the project manager, who will have these key responsibilities:

- ensuring the design consultant has all the information necessary to develop the design
- acting as the first point of contact for the client team
- ensuring decisions are made by the client team and communicating them to the design consultant when required
- taking overall responsibility for budget management, including responsibility for feeding back information to funders
- ensuring the design is agreed and signed off at key stages on behalf of the client team.

The role of the design consultant should be outlined in the detailed brief. They will be required to carry out tasks as outlined in the brief which may include managing community involvement in the design process as well as carrying out the design work.

The Landscape Institute's work stages, set out opposite, provide a useful industry standard to refer to, although the client may need to adapt them to the particular circumstances of a project.

Inception and feasibility stages have been covered in the *Prepare* section of this guide. The extent to which initial outline proposals are needed depends on the complexity of the project. For smaller, less complex projects, it may be appropriate for the consultant to start with sketch scheme proposals. The following section outlines the typical design process from stage D.

Work stages	Preliminary services

A Inception
B Feasibilty

Standard services

C Outline proposals
D Sketch scheme proposals
E Detailed proposals
FG Production information
HJ Tender action and contract preparation
K Operations on site
L Completion

The Landscape Institute, *Engaging a landscape architect consultant: guidance for clients on fees*, 2002

©Groundwork UK

The sketch scheme proposal

58	59	60		62

The design consultant will prepare a sketch scheme proposal in line with the vision and design brief and based on the site survey and analysis of the site. It helps to start this process with a walk around the site with the design consultant to clarify any points in the brief and to document what the site looks like before improvement by taking photographs. It is important to have plans drawn to scale and to ask the designer to provide three-dimensional sketches. Where the budget is sufficient, models of the site or computer generated images can help people better understand the proposal.

The client should take time to understand the proposal and ask questions about it. It is important for stakeholders to see the sketch design as they may also have questions and it may need minor amendment, before showing it to the wider community. It is important to ensure everyone who may use the site or benefit from it is given the opportunity to comment on the plans. It helps to have the design consultant present at meetings to explain the sketch design. Set aside at least a month in the timetable for the designer to carry out this stage.

The sketch design should include:

– cost estimates
– programme for implementation
– size and character of the project shown in plans and sketches
– any necessary application for outline planning permission
– other approvals from statutory bodies.

Adapted from the Landscape Institute, *The landscape consultant's appointment*, 1998.

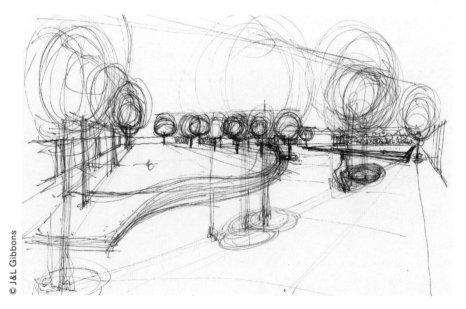

© J&L Gibbons

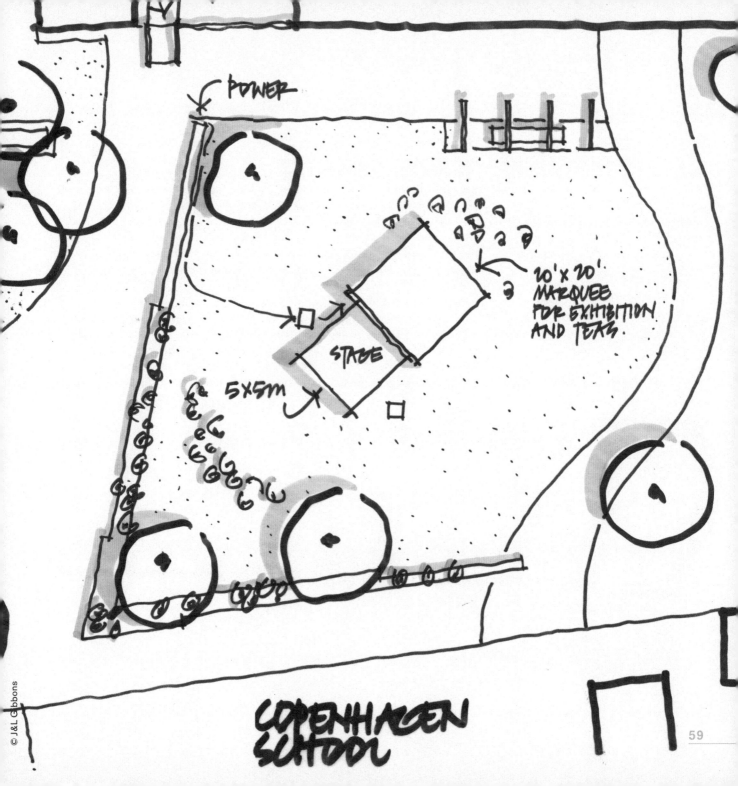

POWER

20' x 20' MARQUEE FOR EXHIBITION AND TEAS

STAGE

5 x 5 m

COPENHAGEN SCHOOL

The detailed proposal

'You should ask your consultant to use models to present certain stages of the project, particularly sketch design...We worked with models throughout the design and presented options for discussion so that the pros and cons of different ideas could be tested at consultation meetings. The advantage of doing this consultation and building the skate area first has been that we have avoided really bad vandalism so far'.

Lynn Kinnear, Kinnear Landscape Architects

Once the sketch scheme proposal is agreed, the detailed proposal can be prepared. This includes a detailed plan of the project, indicating size of features and levels of ground. Depending on the size of the project, the proposal should also include drawn sections through the site showing changes in level; three dimensional sketches and models or computer simulations.

The final plan is the stage where the full cost of the project will be known. It will influence the level of maintenance needed in future, and so its cost. It is important to get signed approval from the key stakeholders involved in the project before proceeding to implement the design. This could take some time to achieve, as people will have specific concerns related to individual aspects of the site. If people's concerns are not resolved, they are likely to raise them again. At this stage, the design should be considered as frozen, that is, any subsequent changes may mean the design consultant can claim extra fees.

© J&L Gibbons

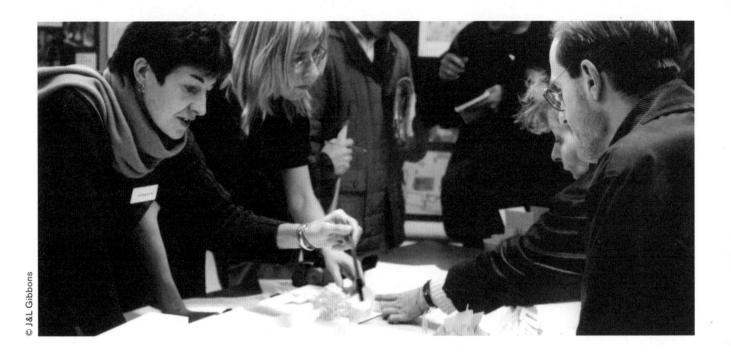

Through a process of collaboration with artists and local schools, the complex aspirations of an inner city community were embodied in the design for Edward Square, London

As well as approvals from the client and stakeholders, the client will need approval from a range of others before the project starts on site. This includes the landowner and it may also be necessary to seek planning approval. It is helpful to have involved a planning officer from the local council in the early stages of the project so that the group can get a feel for the likely outcome of any planning applications. They will be able to advise the client whether the project fulfils aspirations set out in overall design statements and policies for the area.

The detailed design will include:

– proposed materials, techniques and standards of workmanship
– proposals made by other consultants, specialist contractors or suppliers as appropriate
– quotations and other information in relation to specialist work
– changes to the estimated cost and programme
– any necessary applications for detailed planning permission.

Adapted from the Landscape Institute, *The landscape consultant's appointment*, 1998.

The tender documents

Once the detailed proposal is complete and approved by all partners, the next step is for the design consultant to produce detailed tender documents. This is production information, everything the contractor will need to cost and build the project. This will consist of written specifications, planting plans and construction drawings. They will also include specifications for maintenance for pricing by the contractor. Take time to understand the documents that go with this stage, the drawings, specification of works and programme of construction.

The client will need to decide, on the advice of the design consultant, to what extent the contractor that builds the project is tied into maintaining it. Landscape contracts typically include one year's maintenance but to ensure good establishment of the site, up to a three year maintenance period may be preferable. This decision may depend on who will be responsible for maintenance in the long-term and how it is to be funded.

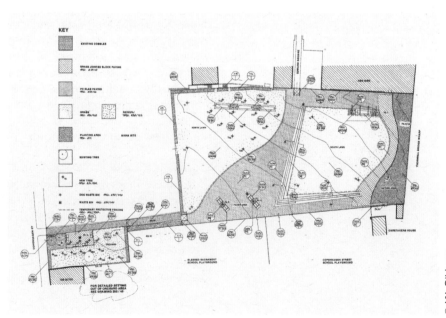

SPACE

Key questions

- Have the client, stakeholders and the community agreed the sketch design?

- Have the client, stakeholders and the community signed off the detailed design?

- Are all necessary approvals in place?

- Has the design consultant prepared the tender documents?

Never lose sight of the vision: Cambridgeshire

Client and partners Gamlingay Parish Council, South Cambridgeshire District Council, Forward Gamlingay! and Gamlingay and District skate park association

Designers civic Architects

Size 0.04 hectares (part of a larger area)

Current stage out to tender September 2006

Cost Estimated £190,000 seeking funding

The Forward Gamlingay! Youth design project is an ambitious contribution to the community life of the village. The team had to work hard not to lose high level design ambitions that were established at the start of the project, and throughout the design process.

Young people in Gamlingay, Cambridgeshire had nowhere to meet, socialise and access services. That became the incentive for a group of local people to set up Forward Gamlingay! - an umbrella group formed from members of the community, in partnership with the local parish and civic Architects. Its chief aim was to improve facilities for teenagers living in the area. With the status of a registered charity, Forward Gamlingay! has developed a joined-up masterplan of all its projects. Key among these are designs for a new skate park and community pavilion, and redeveloping the First school's swimming pool and scout hut. Dan Jones from civic Architects explains the challenge of developing a high quality design vision for the project:

'If you ask people to point out high quality buildings near where they live, they mostly choose historic buildings, like churches or old houses. But when people set out with high level design ambition on present-day projects, they have to fly in the face of all sorts of pressures that try and persuade them to dumb-down their original vision.'

© civic Architects

The architects had made a computer model of the site using 'beat 'em up' computer game software. They created a continuous environment where viewers could move around the proposals as the designs evolved

'If you ask people to point out high quality buildings near where they live, they mostly choose historic buildings, like churches or old houses. But when people set out with high level design ambition on present-day projects, they have to fly in the face of all sorts of pressures that try and persuade them to dumb-down their original vision.'

Dan Jones, civic Architects

© civic Architects

Adjacent local landmarks appeared in the computer model and provided a context against which the scale of proposals could be understood

Following a Glass-House Community Led Design course called Young Spacemakers, the youth team led development of the architects' design to produce an ambitious and inspirational design for a new public space and community pavilion. This intensive involvement has allowed the young people to learn about the value of different spaces, contribute strategically to the design process and establish key design principles. A computer model has enabled the youngsters to be sensitive to spatial issues in developing their brief and make judgements in response to the form and shape of the architects' proposals. The project will move forward when Forward Gamlingay! succeeds in raising capital funds. Five key principles were identified to define the qualities and relationships that the project should embody:

- the design should make links and connections
- the design should create different levels and different types of spaces
- the community pavilion (shelter) should be located with privacy and sociability in mind
- the entire space should relate to the surrounding context, trees, landscape and views
- the shelter should be carefully designed in terms of size, shape and twist.

Forward Gamlingay! Youth design project, *Log book*, 2005

You need to know

The Glass-House Community Led Design community design advisor supported civic Architects throughout the early stages of this project to programme, co-facilitate and document the early design stages. The advisor also helped sustain the demand-led design process and encouraged shared decision-making between the architects and young people. Do not lose sight of high level design ambitions that were established at the start of the project, and throughout the design process. Consider funding at the start of the project to ensure there is not any pressure on design proposals.

See www.forwardgamlingay.com or visit Forward Gamlingay! Church Street, Gamlingay, SG19

Don't compromise on design quality: London

Client and partners Edward Square steering group (now Friends of Edward Square (FREDS)) including: London Borough of Islington planning and education department, The government office for London, Copenhagen school, Blessed sacrament school, York Way court youth group, South Islington Bangladeshi association, the Somali speakers association and the Copenhagen neighbourhood forum

Designers J&L Gibbons Landscape Architects; poet Andrew Motion; artist for lettering, Gary Breeze; artist for wall panel, Kate Blee; education liaison officer and artist Patsy Hans

Size 0.5 hectares

Current stage completed 1996-2000

Cost £301,000 from Single regeneration budget and planning gain

Combined dedication of the community and the designer has resulted in a public space that reflects the high quality of traditional London squares as well as responding to the needs of local people.

Designated as temporary open space and threatened by nearby development, local residents led the campaign to save Edward Square in north London. The steering group appointed a designer early on. After interviewing three candidates with suitable expertise, J&L Gibbons was chosen as the design team. The group asked the designers to consult the local community to try and creatively reconcile their differing interests and needs. It stressed that the design needed to be managed at a relatively low cost.

The designers were given six weeks to complete the feasibility study and develop a sketch design for the funding bid. Negotiating with adjacent landowners about the quality of their development and its relationship to and impact on the square became an ongoing part of their brief. The project was completed a year later including six months for the detailed design.

© J & L Gibbons

The qualities of a typical London square serve as a benchmark for the design, including the majestic scale of mature plane trees, the geometry of the layout and, as a central focus, lawns and perimeter pathways. Other aspirations are to improve the view for the adjacent school, reconstruct links and maintain through routes, while creating a destination

'This was very much a grass roots project, because of the involvement of the community and the skill of the designers. What could have been a bland upgrade, has instead produced a design which has stood the test of time and become a space much loved by the local community.'

Lucy Shomali, policy and projects manager, London Borough of Islington

© J & L Gibbons

Edward Square, Islington, has been awarded a Green Flag Award. The award is a testament to the success of the project and the continued involvement of the Friends of Edward Square

J&L Gibbons supported and promoted the project intensively, in order to achieve a consensus and engender a sense of ownership, especially with local youngsters, to prevent them feeling disenchanted. Significant sweat equity was raised and documented, including planning aid from a barrister, specialist help from the Open Spaces Society and work by members of the steering group with professional skills. The designer and planning officers also made a significant personal commitment to raising expectations, in order to create a memorable place. Lucy Shomali, policy and projects manager, London Borough of Islington, describes the dedication towards the project:

'This was very much a grass roots project, because of the involvement of the community and the skill of the designers. What could have been a bland upgrade, has instead produced a design which has stood the test of time and become a space much loved by the local community.'

A maintenance plan and the dedication of resources for at least 10 years were conditions of funding. The friends group that emerged from the steering committee has been responsible for promoting use of the square, as well as maintenance monitoring. To assist the friends, a dedicated ranger from the council's Green Space team has inspected the square weekly over the past three years. Since the project has been completed, only one wooden seat and some willow stakes have been removed, and a few trees vandalised. After users informally marked out a basketball court, the council was compelled to respond by making the court permanent.

You need to know

Select a design team to develop the design brief according to site-specific needs such as creatively reconciling different interests. Collaboratively set a benchmark for design quality that reflects the context of the area. Aim to involve the designer for up to five years after completion to protect and retain the integrity of the design.

Visit Edward Square in Islington, London N1.

Appoint the construction contractor

'Delivery is the last 15 per cent of the project, but it is the part that people will see and is the legacy of the project.'

Nina Porter, Reigate and Banstead Borough Council

A skilled landscape contractor is required for any project that requires moving earth, constructing walls, paving or operating heavy machinery. They also know how to achieve good planting. Specialist sub-contractors may also be needed to install specialist items such as play equipment or surfaces. The local council's planning department may help with this process or the design consultant can suggest an appropriate method and contractors for the client team to shortlist, usually registered with the British Association of Landscape Industries (BALI) www.bali.co.uk

The client should make sure to check the quality of projects the contractors have worked on before. Once appointed, the client then needs to agree the date to start on site and sign the contract with the construction company. The JCLI Form of Agreement is recognised as the most appropriate to landscape schemes, see www.jcli.org.uk. The contractual agreement will be between the client and the contractor, and there are legal implications of this that the design consultant can advise on.

The design consultant will be familiar with preparing and managing contracts and can act as the client's agent to oversee the contract. Specifically the design consultant should:

- advise on suitable contractors and draw up a tender list
- invite tenders from contractors
- analyse tenders when submitted and advise the client on selection, it may not be the lowest cost
- prepare the contract and arrange for it to be signed by the client and the contractor
- ensure all information is in place for works to start on site.

Opposite: BTCV volunteers rebuilding the walls in Penmaenmawr Memorial Gardens, North Wales

Adapted from the Landscape Institute, *The landscape consultant's appointment*, 1998.

The client will need to be aware of the Construction (Design and Management) regulations 1994, commonly referred to as CDM regulations. These cover the responsibility of a client and contractor during construction for health and safety on site. The design consultant should be able to advise if these apply. In all cases, there will be a need to carry out a risk assessment at the design stage.

Use the construction process as a learning opportunity

Opposite: Volunteers on a BTCV training course learning the craft of hedge laying on public open space on the outskirts of Barnsley, South Yorkshire

As well as the skilled landscape contractor, the project could involve trainees, volunteers, children and young people. Training schemes are often looking for projects for their students to work on and this option provides semi-skilled labour, for example, through a youth offending team. Organisations such as BTCV can also offer semi-skilled pairs of hands. They will charge a daily rate but can give useful advice, including the cost of insuring volunteers working on site. As the client team may still have to provide equipment, machine hire and on-site facilities, it could well cost the same as a commercial contractor. The same is true of volunteers, children and young people. There would not only be the added responsibility for their health and safety, but the timescales would have to be relaxed. The benefit, however, lies in involving local people, creating a sense of ownership and adding to their skills, and it may also be recorded as a benefit in kind. In other words, human resources and other gifts can be counted as match funding, if required.

Start work on site

Once the contractor starts work on the site the client's vision starts to become a reality. This is an exciting stage of the project but it may disrupt the use of the site for some time. It is important to keep local people informed. This can be done through temporary signage which explains the project and the construction timescale, or regular meetings to keep the community informed of the progress.

The construction period is the stage most likely to be subject to delays in progress and increases in cost. This is the reason for building contingencies into the budget at an early stage. It is important for the client to control costs and keep records of money contributed to the project and money spent in order to report back to funders.

The creation of Gardd y Coleg community park, in Carmel, Wales, is a means of providing a focal point for the community. Not only to accomplish a pleasing, visual transformation of the environment but also to forge and strengthen bonds between members of the community

© Alan Patterson

Top: A recess was dug out by volunteers allowing two other volunteers to construct a stone wall to complement the same type of construction on the opposite side of the path, using reclaimed stone

Above: A mini digger and dumper were hired, along with the services of two drivers. Tons of topsoil were removed from the picnic area and the site was levelled out. The topsoil was carried to the parking area and a price was negotiated with the car park contractor who expressed an interest in purchasing the material. The machines were also used to carry slate waste to the picnic area and levelled out as a sub-base. The grano was transported in the same way to cover the footpaths

Left: S4C's Clwb Garddio, the Welsh Gardener's World, arrived to film the official opening of the garden. It was opened by broadcaster Gerallt Pennant and around 200 people visited the garden on the day

Doorstep Greens © Natural England

Once the works have started on site the design consultant, if employed to act as the client's agent, will oversee the contract. This will typically include:

- site visits to inspect the progress and quality
- checking and certifying the contractor's payments
- keeping track of construction costs and keep the client informed
- agreeing with the client that works are satisfactorily complete.

Adapted from the Landscape Institute, *The landscape consultant's appointment*, 1998.

As the project progresses it is important to keep people informed

Project handover

On completion of works on site the client should ask the design consultant to prepare a handover manual which should include all the as-constructed drawings, warranties, information about suppliers and instructions on any equipment built into the site. This information will be vital for managing the site in the future to the original design.

SPACE

Key questions

- Has the contractor been appointed to construct the site?

- Has risk been considered fully?

- Is a proper process in place to monitor stages of construction?

- Has the local community been informed of what is happening on site?

- Has the group retained all the necessary information needed for future management of the site?

Gain professional support: London

Client and partners Mapesbury Conservation Area Trust, Mapesbury Residents' Association, London Borough of Brent Parks Service

Designers CMS Design Associates

Size 0.2 hectares

Current stage completed 2000-2005

Cost £165,000 from Doorstep Greens programme and Living Spaces

Sustainability and best value for money were key criteria in selecting the construction contractor for this project. To achieve this, professional support was gained from the council's parks service.

Situated in Brent, north west London, Mapesbury Dell had fallen into disrepair. Although it was a unique pocket in an area of few public open spaces, not surprisingly, it was underused. The client team was established as a subgroup of an already strong residents' association. The London Borough of Brent's Parks Service provided help with cost planning, technical and project management prior to and during construction. It also advised on the more complex decision-making processes. Consultants conducted extensive public consultation.

Catharina Malmberg-Snodgrass, a local resident and award-winning landscape designer, was willing to give her time without a fee. The trust asked the designer for creative ideas to resolve tensions that emerged during consultation and how to involve volunteers in the upkeep of the park. She developed a design proposal, in line with the detailed brief. The trust made sure that she exercised impartiality in developing the design, accommodating the main objectives identified through consultation.

From the final design, Brent Parks Service prepared a Bill of Quantities and a tender specification for construction. The client evaluated tenders from 12 specialist landscape contractors and chose the one offering the best value

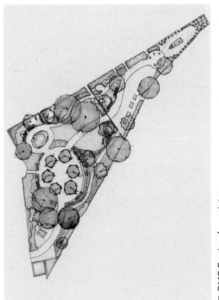

© CMS Design Associates

Main objectives identified through consultation were reflected in the concept design, such as a play area for families with young children and quiet seating areas for contemplation and relaxation

© CMS Design Associates

Brent Parks Service evaluated the design for its sustainability and made adjustments accordingly. Materials such as gravel paving which minimise water run-off and mulching to retain moisture were used

for money. Brent Parks Service, which underwrote the project, managed it on site and was therefore able to monitor costs during construction.

To develop the project plan and proposal the client collected small donations from residents and seed funding from the Doorstep Greens programme. In addition to the grant funding, monies were raised through the Parks Service annual capital and revenue accounts, and the Parks Service underwrote the project to ensure that there was no shortfall in funding. This process took over a year to conclude. At least a further 20 per cent of the budget was contributed through sweat equity: design and project management services given in kind.

The trust established an 80-year agreement with Brent Parks Service to provide basic maintenance and set up a gardening club to carry out special maintenance. Ease of maintenance was a key consideration. The Mapesbury Dell website explains how the space will continue to improve: 'The Dell is not a static item. It's alive and we want to keep it that way! While the current programme of works will give us a wonderful local park, we look on this as a good beginning, rather than the end of the works. So, future improvements are already in hand.' Selected semi-mature trees and shrubs were chosen to be focal points together with very young and less expensive plant material. Hardwearing furniture was chosen to add to the site's environmental sustainability.

You need to know

Initially, the brief had suggested installing CCTV cameras to make the park feel safer. Instead, improved security has been achieved practically rather than technically through changing the hours of use, promoting natural surveillance and improving circulation. The site is approached by a single alleyway and has one entrance, posing challenges for being a truly public space accessible to everyone. Artwork by Jim Partridge and Liz Walmsley has been installed for a more interesting and welcoming entrance.

See www.mapesbury-dell.org or visit Mapesbury Dell, Hoveden Road, London NW2.

Harness skills in the community: Cornwall

Client and partners St Neot Parish Council, Duchy of Cornwall Nurseries, Cornwall County Council

Designers Hunt Winter Architects, Tracy Wilson, Duchy of Cornwall Nurseries

Size 0.45 hectares

Current stage completed 2000-2005

Cost £80,000 from the Doorstep Greens Programme and St Neot Parish Council, supplemented by 2,000 volunteer hours and low cost supplies from local traders.

Developing skills within the community has united a village and maximised funds for this project. The outcome is a new amenity in which the revived community spirit can thrive.

Despite being right at the centre of the village, St Neot Doorstep Green was cut off from the main movement networks. A local landowner gave the green to the parish to be developed for the community to use as a bowling green and tennis court. However, an early feasibility study showed that creating the level surfaces needed on a sloping site next to a river would be technically problematic and far too expensive. Instead, the parish council drew up a proposal for an informal garden with a variety of recreational uses. This proved popular so the project was developed in more detail.

The new vision for the site retained the sense of civic purpose of the original bequest but suggested uses which would draw in a wider cross-section of the village community. A local architect was commissioned to develop the spatial arrangement of the site, incorporating the community's ideas. These included comments generated from a further consultation exhibition at the local school.

Images: *Doorstep Greens* © Natural England

'Over 2,000 volunteer hours went into working on the project with over 1,600 trees and shrubs being planted by our willing band of helpers. The amphitheatre was built in just 10 working days, mostly at weekends, with some 40 different workers lending a hand. It is also guesstimated that in the region of 300 pasties were polished off during the lunch breaks.'

St Neot Parish Council, www.stneot.org.uk, 2005

The parish council appointed a project manager who combined project management with design and horticultural skills. A main contractor built the substructure for the green, excavating, grading and constructing footpath bases. Then volunteers, with the advice of skilled craftspeople including stonemasons, laid paving and built the amphitheatre using stone from the local quarry. They also planted about 1,500 trees and shrubs.

Derek Fairhall, resident, explains: 'Making the green led to people getting to know one another, new friendships were formed at the same time as the quality of life in the village was improved for everyone.'

The client team handed over the green on completion to the Friends of St Neot Doorstep Green, a steering group that took on responsibility for managing the reconstructed space. It has decided to contract maintenance to the council, but seasonal pruning will be carried out by the friends. They fund this activity with a modest income from events on the site.

You need to know

Relying on volunteer labour to such an extent requires considerable co-ordination and can potentially delay a project. A horticulturalist worked collaboratively with the architect to improve the layout, making the design more effective. The determination to address the poor access to the site resulted in creating a new social space at the centre of the village and making new links across it.

See www.countryside.gov.uk or visit St Neot Doorstep Green, Cornwall P146.

Celebrate the opening

Opening event

Organise a grand opening when the project is finished. Make sure any permissions, and if needed, licences are in place from landowners, and make arrangements for the space to be cleaned up afterwards. The client might wish to ask the St. John's Ambulance to provide support on the day, see www.sja.org.uk. Funders and a local councillor or mayor may want to say something and involving them will help to keep the project in their thoughts.

© Northern Echo

What will draw people to the space? Find out if there is a local celebrity or band that would be interested and check local theatres and venues for people performing in the area who may offer a celebrity endorsement. Invite everyone who has already voiced an interest and been involved. Target others through a press release to the local media, including newspapers and radio stations. Have alternative plans in place for wet weather and try to estimate likely numbers, so that the event can be scaled accordingly.

Final completion

Maintenance period

'We would always prefer to be involved but as a private practice we can only stay involved for the time we are paid for, which is usually the defects liability period. It might help on some schemes if designers could be retained in a longer-term role but it would always be hard to justify consultants fees versus spending what is usually a limited amount of money on the best built product for a community.'

Steve Warren, Estell Warren

The relationship with the contractor doesn't usually finish when the works are completed on site. It takes time to see whether works have been completed to a satisfactory standard because some faults don't appear immediately. Most contracts have a defects liability period of at least 12 months, during which the contractor is responsible for any failures in construction and planting. The design consultant should be employed to check the works at the end of the defects liability period. Many designers also like to stay involved in a project long after it has been implemented, and may choose to visit the space and feedback any issues to the group. However, a more secure way to ensure their professional input is retained is to include a maintenance period for up to five years in their contract. This can be cost-effective in ensuring build quality and making sure that management and maintenance is carried out effectively.

It is often difficult to foresee how a site will work in operation once the site is handed over to the client. New sites can attract a lot of users which can cause wear and tear at this particularly vulnerable early stage. The contractor can't be held responsible for any damage to the site in use. The client will need to think about how to fund any works to make good any damage that may happen. This is key to ensuring the site is kept in good condition and is respected by users. At the end of the defects liability period the contractor's role is completed, unless a longer maintenance period is agreed. It's at this stage the management plan takes over as the guiding document for the site.

A forthcoming CABE Space research report on risk and the design of public space, recommends designers consider the possibility of using phased designs to allow learning about potential risks relating to the site prior to completion. This can in turn inform the maintenance and management arrangements for the site

Doorstep Greens © Natural England

Establish management and maintenance

When a project is completed, it begins a new chapter of continuous management, maintenance and improvement. The client team should have already thought about caring for the space at the preparation and design stages.

Prepare a management statement or plan

A management plan or statement helps to manage, maintain, develop and improve the space in the best way. Management plans are also needed to secure funding from certain funding streams and to win an award, such as the Green Flag Award. The thinking that goes into the management plan is as important as the product at the end of it. It should cover at least five years, if not 10 years or more. This plan can be written as part of commissioning the design of the space to make sure it is well cared for afterwards.

Key questions to ask when preparing a management plan or statement for an outdoor space:

- where are we now? An introduction, wider policy context and site description
- where do we want to get to? Vision, assessment and analysis, aims and objectives
- how will we get there? Work/action plan, finance and resources
- how will we know when we have arrived? Monitor and review.

CABE Space, *A guide to producing park and green space management plans*, 2004

A conservation management plan may be needed if the space is a special heritage asset. At the centre of this is understanding the value of the space to people. A specialist would usually be involved and a range of stakeholders consulted in its preparation, see www. hlf.org.uk

Choose levels of involvement

'There is a huge under-exploited potential for people to be involved in the management, maintenance and care of public space. Just imagine if in a typical street all the residents invested in the public realm just what they planned to spend on their bathrooms and kitchens that year? We need to find ways to encourage this and mechanisms to support it.'

Ben Hamilton-Baillie, Hamilton-Baillie Associates

If the landowner is the local council, an agreement will be needed with them to carry out litter removal and other tasks that they have a legal duty to carry out. This agreement should be in place for a minimum of 25 years and ideally for 80 years or more to make sure it is built into long-term plans. Alternatively, if the group owns the site, it will require a paid contract with the council or a private contractor that the client will monitor.

Many of the projects featured in this guide have included an exceptional level of hands on involvement in aftercare by local people, but there are hundreds of other projects that cannot sustain a high level of activity on a day-to-day basis. It can be time consuming to organise, although rewarding in building community spirit and citizenship. Consider whether it is better to pay a private contractor or to form an agreement with a youth offending team or other semi-skilled workforce, such as provided by BTCV.

Decide on opening times

The client team will need to decide on the best approach to making the space accessible to the public. A public space is for everyone and simply fortifying the site with barriers can encourage bad behaviour by presenting a challenge. Moreover, it may make it difficult for people to get out of the space if threatened with harm. Decide what is appropriate, according to the scale of the public space (everyone can go there); to semi-public space (only certain groups of people can go there and at certain times).

Sometimes, the designer will take a strong stance and at Tavistock Gardens the scheme's architect was adamant that the re-designed space should remain open at night. Sarah Harrison from PRP Architects says: 'By keeping it open all the time, the park would become a public place and be easier to police. This shows how sometimes you have to stick to a strong design principle and not give in to residents' wishes'[6]

6 *Regeneration and Renewal magazine*
  1 June, 2005

© Notting Hill Housing Trust

Evaluate the project

It is important to evaluate the project and set and measure standards long after the new space has been opened and the debris of the opening event has been cleared. This will ensure the space stays looking good and working well. The client or a specially nominated group should monitor whether the project has met its original objectives and whether the process went smoothly. This is the time to reflect back and learn lessons for any future projects. The group may wish to set some future objectives at this point, and make sure these are reflected in the management plan for the site. Ideally some key information was collected at the beginning of the project, for example numbers of people using the space and their satisfaction with it, as well as local crime statistics. It is valuable to continue to collect this information, not least as it may be useful for future funding applications. Doing so will be helpful for drawing up an annual action plan within a longer-term management plan. See *Contacts* for other useful tools to evaluate projects.

© Elizabeth Hoehnke

CABE Space has developed Spaceshaper, a tool to measure the quality of public space for use by community groups and professionals

Keep the momentum going

'Our projects are often published or attract design awards and this gives the client added value and more security about what they have got.'

Lynn Kinnear, Kinnear Landscape Architects

'It's about dedication, and I guess I'm a bit of a nutcase really, I've been there six years and I don't see it ending. Every year there's a new challenge, a new wave of kids causing trouble. But every year I win.'

Barbara Wilson

A number of projects featured in this guide have benefited from awards recognising design quality, community involvement and even the efforts of an individual. Some of these are made nationally or regionally and the group may be invited to a ceremony which is a great opportunity to talk to people from other successful projects. Others reflect local success and may be undertaken by the local council.

Take time to read the criteria for award schemes to decide which may be appropriate.

Relevant award schemes include:

– Civic Trust Awards are given to special examples of architecture and environmental design in the UK and consider the benefit of the project to its local area and community as well as the quality of its design www.civictrust.org.uk
– The Green Pennant Award recognises high quality green spaces in England and Wales that are managed by voluntary or community groups www.greenflagaward.org.uk
– The Landscape Institute Awards are design awards with a community category www.landscapeinstitue.org
– Britain in Bloom Awards are made at a local level through regional heats www.rhs.org.uk

© Manchester Evening News

In 2005, Barbara Wilson was awarded the MBE for her services to Coalshaw Green Park in Oldham

SPACE

Key questions

- Has a celebration opening event taken place?

- Is a management plan in place?

- Has the project been evaluated and any actions taken?

- Have you taken the time to put your feet up and enjoy your space?!

Tell us about your experiences of being a community client. Contact enquiries@cabe.org.uk and mark your communication *It's our space*. Share your experiences with others and continue your learning. GreenSpace provides a network of community groups with a shared interest in green spaces and offers training and publications, see www.green-space.org.uk

Living Streets has a network of local branches and individual local campaigners working in their own communities to create living streets, see www.livingstreets.org.uk

Civic Societies are voluntary organisations promoting high standards of planning, conservation and regeneration for the benefit of their local community, see www.civictrust.org.uk

Consider management from the start: London

Client and partners Manor House Users Group, London Borough of Lewisham, Lewisham Police Crime Screening Unit, Glendale Grounds Management

Designers Land Use Consultants

Size 3.5 hectares

Timescale 1993-2000

Cost £2 million from Heritage Lottery Fund, matched by the London Borough of Lewisham

During the design process the client made it explicit that management and maintenance must achieve the national standard for parks and green spaces. Delivery was nevertheless a challenge and ultimately the private sector brought resources that the council was not able to dedicate.

The Grade II listed Manor House Gardens in Lewisham, London was originally built as part of a private estate in the late 18th century, opening as a public park in 1902. Despite its grand beginnings, over time a period of decline set in that continued until 1993, when the London Borough of Lewisham launched a plan to improve it.

A dedicated group emerged from the first meeting held by the council. It was greatly helped by John Hopkins, a local resident and well-respected landscape architect, who acted as a design advocate. As a result the group realised it needed a costed masterplan, based on historical research and contemporary user needs, to form the basis for funding applications. The council paid for development of the design and appointed an officer to act as project manager. Out of six consultants invited to submit tenders, council officers and members of the user group chose Land Use Consultants. Their decision was based on the quality of the bids plus the value they offered.

© Land Use Consultants

Glendale Grounds Management takes pride in the attention to detail given to its development of the site, and is working towards retaining its Green Flag status

'The designer must have flexibility, patience but above all
the courage and conviction to retain design integrity.'

Adrian Wikeley, Land Use Consultants

© Land Use Consultants

Once a privately owned house and grounds,
Manor House Gardens now offers visitors a rare
glimpse of outer London before the late 19th
century expansion of the metropolis

Land Use Consultants led a series of workshops to develop the design
brief. These became a forum to engage people in making decisions
about the design as it progressed from strategy through to detail.
Throughout the process, the design team evaluated to what extent the
design and restoration could be environmentally sustainable. Four months
later, the steering group gave the final proposals their blessing, and
subsequently published the landscape strategy and management plan.
Adrian Wikeley, the design consultant, explains:

'The designer must have flexibility, patience but above all the courage
 and conviction to retain design integrity.'

Community engagement and a 10-year commitment to manage the park
were conditions of the Heritage Lottery Fund bid. In the year before the
gardens finally opened, the council let a management and maintenance
contract to Glendale Grounds Management for 12 parks. The contractor is
committed to quality management and maintenance and has established an
on-site base for its operations. As a result Manor House Gardens has been
able to retain the Green Flag Award for the past four years.

You need to know

Long-term commitment is needed for projects of this size and nature.
In this case it took four years for funds to be raised and seven years for the
management to be established. At the same time, the design strategy should
be characterised by a thorough professional understanding of the place.
The design consultant may need to convince the community client and users
that the concept will work, is worthy of being funded and will deliver the
benefits that they want.

See www.lewisham.co.uk or visit Manor House Gardens, Manor Lane,
London SE13

Use a space as a catalyst: Manchester

Client and partners Albion Residents' Association, Charlestown
& Lower Kersal New Deal for Communities

Design Groundwork Manchester, Salford & Trafford; mural and
sculptures by Action Factory; traversing wall by Bendcrete

Size 0.07 hectares

Timescale completed February – May 2005

Cost £82,000 from New Deal for Communities, European Regional
Development Fund (ERDF), Market Renewal Fund, Awards for All and
Living Spaces

In February 2005, the Albion Residents' Association was awarded first prize in the government's competition to find England's top community space project, a reward for their dedication to improving their neighbourhood.

After some flats on the corner of Gerald Road and Seaford Road, Salford, had been demolished the land was left derelict for years. The New Deal for Communities (NDC) team led a neighbourhood planning consultation. Subsequently, residents from the Albion estate approached Groundwork Manchester, Salford and Trafford asking for help in turning the plot of land into a community garden.

The community link officer from Groundwork worked closely with the community to capture their aspirations for the site, taking them to visit other similar projects to provide ideas. Jacki Henderson, one of Groundwork's landscape architects, was also brought in to work with the residents and develop a design based on their wish list. She proposed introducing works of art, such as sculptures and murals and put the commission to make the artworks out to tender.

The garden is on the site of a former dog track and building on its history the theme of dogs in the neighbourhood formed the basis for the design.

© Groundwork Manchester, Salford and Trafford

A ribbon cutting ceremony marked the official opening of Albion Community Garden on 7 May 2005

'The project is a wonderful example of a whole community coming together and making their neighbourhood a cleaner, safer and greener place to live in. What particularly impressed me was that residents of all ages got stuck in to the tidy up, whether it was the youngsters picking up the litter or the older people who helped with the planting.'[7]   Phil Hope, Minister, Office of the Deputy Prime Minister (ODPM)

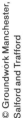

© Groundwork Manchester, Salford and Trafford

Dog models made by members of Albion Residents' Association were the basis for sculptures incorporated into the garden

The residents were also keen to involve children of all ages in exercise and play within the site. All these ideas inspired a unique community garden which contains unusual sculptures of dogs, a traversing wall cleverly incorporated into a colourful wall mural made up of local dog stories, play markings, raised planters, an open grassed area, benches and a picnic table. The garden is secured by a fence with lockable gates which is opened by community key holders and stays open until dusk.

The garden's transformation was so remarkable, that it was entered into the local 'In Bloom' competition. It also won the government's Picture of Change competition in 2005 which will enhance the group's work, including another local project to tackle graffiti with a large scale mural project. Presenting the award Phil Hope, then parliamentary under-secretary of state in the Office of the Deputy Prime Minister (ODPM), said:

'The project is a wonderful example of a whole community coming together and making their neighbourhood a cleaner, safer and greener place to live in. What particularly impressed me was that residents of all ages got stuck in to the tidy up, whether it was the youngsters picking up the litter or the older people who helped with the planting.'[7]

———————————

7 ODPM news release, www.communities.gov.uk, 2005.

You need to know

The project was completed in 2005 and given the pressures of use, being adjacent to a row of neighbourhood shops, it is exceptionally tidy and shows minimal signs of wear and tear.

Visit Albion Community Garden in Manchester, M6.

Checklist of key stages

The following checklist outlines the key stages of a project.
Tick off each stage as they are completed:

Prepare

- Establish the client team and roles ☐
- Establish a partnership ☐
- Identify, consult and involve people ☐
- Understand the site ☐
- Secure funding ☐
- Appoint the design consultant ☐
- Develop a vision for the site ☐
- Develop the brief ☐

Design

- The sketch scheme proposal ☐
- The detailed proposal ☐
- The tender documents ☐

Construct

- Appoint the construction contractor ☐
- Use the construction process as a learning opportunity ☐
- Start work on site ☐

Use

- Celebrate the opening ☐
- Final completion ☐
- Establish management and maintenance ☐
- Evaluate the project ☐
- Keep the momentum going. ☐

Contacts

Architecture Centre Network

The Architecture Centre Network (ACN) is the national voice for the UK's 22 Architecture Centres. The ACN actively supports, connects and advances the work of the centres to secure greater knowledge, access, participation and influence at all levels, in the creation of an excellent built environment for all. www.architecturecentre.net

BTCV

BTCV is a unique international volunteering organisation providing the bridge between global environmental ideals and local reality in the UK and overseas. www2.btcv.org.uk

Big Lottery Fund

Big Lottery Fund is responsible for giving out half the money for good causes raised by the National Lottery, with a budget of about £630 million a year. Funding covers health, education, environment and charitable purposes. They are committed to bringing real improvements to communities and the lives of people most in need. BIG's Changing Spaces programme is supporting rural and urban environment projects in England. www.biglotteryfund.org.uk

Charity Commission

The Charity Commission is established by law as the regulator and registrar for charities in England and Wales. Their aim is to provide the best possible regulation of charities in England and Wales in order to increase charities' effectiveness and public confidence and trust. www.charitycommission.gov.uk

Civic Trust

The Civic Trust inspires and promotes improvements in the quality of urban life for everyone throughout the UK. It is devoted to enhancing the quality of life in Britain's cities, towns and villages: the places where people live, work, shop and relax. It also sets high standards of design, management and sustainability, and recognises and rewards the best with its annual Civic Trust Awards and the Green Flag Awards. www.civictrust.org.uk

Communities and Local Government

Communities and Local Government was created on 5 May 2006, under the leadership of Ruth Kelly. Their vision is of prosperous and cohesive communities, offering a safe, healthy and sustainable environment for all. Their role is to build the capacity of communities to shape and protect their own future. www.communities.gov.uk

Companies House

The main functions of Companies House are to incorporate and dissolve limited companies; examine and store company information delivered under the Companies Act and related legislation; and make this information available to the public. www.companieshouse.gov.uk

Countryside Agency

The Countryside Agency now forms part of Natural England it was the statutory champion and watchdog that brings together all the different countryside dimensions – economic, environmental, community and enjoyment – into a single national body: to achieve sustainable development in the countryside. www.countryside.gov.uk

Development Trusts Association

Development Trusts Association is the national body for development trusts. The aim of the Development Trusts Association (DTA) is a successful development trust in every community that wants one. The primary work of the DTA is the promotion and exchange of practitioner skills and experience. DTA also joins with others to attract investment and support for the community enterprise movement. www.dta.org.uk

ENCAMS (Environmental Campaigns)

ENCAMS is the independent national charity that runs the Keep Britain Tidy Campaign, Blue Flag Awards for clean beaches and the Eco-Schools programme. They aim to get people to stop dropping litter – and use a bin. They also campaign on issues such as graffiti, flyposting, abandoned vehicles and fly-tipping. www.encams.org

England's Community Forests

There are 12 Community Forests in England, each located in and around a major urban area. Half of England's population lives in or within easy reach of a Community Forest. Their task is to deliver a comprehensive package of urban, economic and social regeneration, creating high-quality environments for millions of people by revitalising derelict land, providing new opportunities for leisure, recreation, and cultural activities, enhancing biodiversity and supporting education, healthy living and social and economic development. www.communityforest.og.uk

Federation of City Farms and Community Gardens (FCFCG)

The Federation of City Farms and Community Gardens is a charity that supports, promotes and represents city farms and community gardens throughout the UK. Its members range from organic orchards to pockets of urban space saved from development; from allotment associations to well established city farms. There are 59 city farms, over 1,000 community gardens, 66 school farms and many allotment groups. www.farmgarden.org.uk

Glass-House Community Led Design

The Glass-House is a national charity offering free design advice, training and project support to tenant, resident and community groups involved in physical regeneration projects and bespoke services to design and regeneration professionals. The Glass-House programmes enable community groups to work collaboratively with professionals and agencies to increase opportunities for more inclusive and better informed regeneration projects with a high standard of design. www.theglasshouse.org.uk

Green Flag Award scheme

The Green Flag Award scheme is the national standard for parks and green spaces throughout England and Wales. The scheme is a means of recognising and rewarding the best green spaces in the country and thus seen as a way of encouraging others to achieve the same high environmental standards. Awards are given on an annual basis and winners must apply each year to renew their Green Flag status. www.greenflagaward.org.uk

Green Pennant Award

The Green Pennant Award is part of the Green Flag Award scheme. It recognises and rewards high quality green spaces in England and Wales that are managed by community or voluntary groups. Sites are assessed against eight criteria, including community involvement. Judging is based on a site visit, and successful sites are eligible to fly a pennant for the year. www.greenflagaward.org.uk

GreenSpace (formerly Urban Parks Forum)

GreenSpace is a charitable organisation set up to help those committed to the planning, design, management and use of public parks and open spaces. It is a membership organisation dedicated to promoting the importance of public spaces and increasing awareness of related issues. www.green-space.org.uk

Green Space Learning network

The Green Space Learning network is facilitated by Natural England's Doorstep Greens team, but works with all partners to help the network become a vital hub for the future. Aims of the network are to provide a resource base for people who are managing green spaces close to people's homes and to give an arena to professionals who work in green space management to discuss and debate. www.greenspace.net.countryside.gov.uk

GreenSTAT

GreenSTAT is a system that gives local residents the opportunity to comment on the quality of their open spaces and how well they feel they are being managed and maintained. It allows site managers to compare the results with others up and down the country to give a truly national voice of what people think about open spaces. www.greenstat.org.uk

Groundwork UK

Groundwork is a federation of Trusts in England, Wales and Northern Ireland, each working with their partners to improve the quality of the local environment, the lives of local people and the success of local businesses in areas in need of investment and support. www.groundwork.org.uk

Heritage Lottery Fund

The Heritage Lottery Fund helps groups and organisations of all sizes with projects that aim to conserve and enhance the UK's diverse heritage and encourages more people to learn about, be involved in, and make decisions about their heritage. Heritage includes many different things and places. Among these are the countryside, parks and gardens; objects and sites that are linked to our industrial, transport and maritime history; records such as local history archives, photographic collections or oral history; historic buildings; and museum and gallery collections. www.hlf.org.uk

Landscape Institute

The Landscape Institute is the chartered institute for landscape architects in the UK. It promotes the highest standards in the practice of landscape architecture and management. Its main objective is to regulate the way its members operate through its mandatory code of professional conduct. www.landscapeinstitute.org

Living Streets

Living Streets is a UK based campaigning charity, working for better streets and public spaces for people on foot. Living Streets works on practical projects with the aim of creating safe, vibrant and healthy streets for all, and has a network of local branches which campaign at a local level. As part of their charity, Living Streets provide consultancy services, working with local authorities and private consultancies, to assess and improve the 'walkability' of streets and public spaces. www.livingstreets.org.uk

National Playing Fields Association (NPFA)

The NPFA is the only national organisation with specific responsibility for acquiring, protecting and improving playing fields and play space. It provides an advisory service and publications on design, layout and safety. www.npfa.org

Natural England

Natural England brings together and builds on the strengths of the Rural Development Service, English Nature and The Landscape, Access and Recreation Division of the Countryside Agency. The new organisation has responsibility for enhancing biodiversity, landscapes and wildlife, promoting access, recreation and public wellbeing and contributing to the way natural resources are managed so sites can be enjoyed now and in the future. www.naturalengland.co.uk

New Economics Foundation (nef)

The New Economics Foundation (nef) is an independent 'think-and-do' tank. nef challenges mainstream thinking on economic, environmental and social issues with innovative ideas, research and advocacy and runs practical projects so that individuals can improve their own lives. nef believes in economics as if people and the planet mattered. www.neweconomics.org

RSPB (Royal Society for the Protection of Birds)

The RSPB is the UK charity working to secure a healthy environment for birds and all wildlife, helping to create a better world for everyone. www.rspb.org.uk

Sustrans

Sustrans works on practical projects to encourage people to walk, cycle and use public transport in order to reduce motor traffic. It is responsible for the National Cycle Network, a project that has delivered nearly 10,000 miles of routes in the UK. www.sustrans.org.uk

Tree Council

The Tree Council is an umbrella body which works for effective action for trees in towns, cities and the countryside and to make them matter to everyone. Goals include more trees, of the right kind and in the right places, and better care for all trees. www.treecouncil.org.uk

Trees for Cities

Trees for Cities is an independent charity that works with local communities on tree planting projects. www.treeforcities.org

The Wildlife Trusts

The Wildlife Trusts is the UK's largest charity exclusively dedicated to conserving all our habitats and species. It comprises a network of 47 local Wildlife Trusts across the UK that work together to protect wildlife in towns and the countryside. www.wildlifetrusts.org

Waste Watch

Waste Watch is the leading national organisation promoting and encouraging action on the 3Rs - waste reduction, reuse and recycling. www.wastewatch.org.uk

Glossary

The following terms are included here in case clients meet them in the course of a project. Definitions are not set in stone and in some cases slightly different meanings are given to them.

Accessibility
The ease with which a building, place or facility can be reached by people and/or goods and services

Adaptability
The capacity of a space or building to respond to changing social, environmental and economic needs

Aspiration
A desired goal or objective

Benefit/s in kind
These are benefits, excluding salaries, given to projects which include volunteer time, materials and services

Biodiversity
The variety and genetic range of forms of life around us from mammals and birds to plants and microbes and the habitat they live in

Biodiversity action plan
A set of proposals and steps required to promote and facilitate biodiversity, usually written by a local council

Cadastre
A register of the ownership of a site, including its boundaries, owners and value

Community strategy
A strategy which a local council has a duty to prepare, setting out a long-term vision that has been agreed with all the main local stakeholders, including public, private and community sector organisations, through a local strategic partnership

Construction drawings
Drawings that set out vital information including dimensions, specifications and layout about the way in which a building or structure should be constructed

Defects liability period
The immediate period following the completion of a project during which the responsibility for remedying any defects identified normally lies with the contractor

Demographics
The statistical data of a population usually identifying trends and averages

Environmental impact assessment
The measurement of the effect a development has on the environment, for example loss of wildlife or erosion

Feasibility study
A review undertaken by a professional team to check whether a set of proposals is likely to be achieved with regard to its design, timing and cost

Funding streams
Sources of finance for a project

Green corridors
A green corridor is a green space that runs through a town or local area often made up of a continuous chain of parks, recreation grounds, woodland and other green spaces

Grid pattern
A design pattern made up of a network of uniformly spaced and intersecting horizontal and perpendicular lines usually relating to a network of streets or housing layout

Hydrology
The patterns of flow and distribution of water on a site, both above and below surface

Inclusiveness
The degree to which a project, space or community includes a variety of types of users, residents and stakeholders preventing separation and reducing social barriers

Incorporated company
A company that is formed and maintained as a legal corporation

Incremental design
Designing gradually in small stages

Legibility
The ability of a place to be easily understood by its users, and ease to find one's way around and how to use it

Management plan or statement
A detailed report outlining the expectations, aspirations, objectives and priorities for the continued management of a space or project. This also includes details of a process for monitoring and evaluating progress

Masterplan
A design that sets out the framework and vision for a large area such as a neighbourhood or district, providing a context for individual projects

Match funding
Funding that is found by groups to match, pound for pound, the size of a grant that has been offered by a funding organisation. It is often a requirement to qualify for grant approval

Open tendering process
A process of advertising an open invitation for organisations/contractors to submit a proposal, with costs, to carry out a piece of work, it covers the preliminary invitation to tender, formal invitation to tender and the actual form of tender

Participatory appraisal
The process whereby designers and a community or user group work in partnership to determine the worth and effectiveness of something; usually a project that impacts upon the community

Perspective
A drawing showing a view from a particular point as it would be seen by a person in the space

Place-making
The process of developing a distinct identity for a place

Planning for Real ©
This is a registered trade mark of the Neighbourhood Initiatives Foundation. It is a method of community involvement in planning and development focusing on the construction and use of flexible cardboard models and priority cards. The Foundation trains people to use Planning for Real. See www.nif.co.uk

Procurement
The process of buying in goods or services from an external provider

Public realm
All zones/areas that everyone has ready, free and legal access at all times

Radiating paths
These are paths that extend in straight lines from a centre

Robustness
The property of being strongly and firmly built

Seed funding
This is funding often provided by investors to develop a concept and launch the initial stages of a project

Service level agreement
This is a formal written agreement made between the service provider and the service recipient that defines a specified level of service, and/or penalty provisions for services not provided

Sightline
The direct line of vision from a viewer to an object at a position within a space

Soft landscape elements
These are landscape features that are made up of trees, shrubs and other planting

Stakeholders
People or groups that have an investment, share or interest in an organisation or project

Sweat equity
This is a measurable benefit to a project of the labour and effort of others eg community members or professionals

Sustainability
To maintain a process or activity into the future without adverse social, economic or environmental impacts

Tender specification
A detailed description of requirements usually prescribing dimensions, materials and quality of work for a proposed or required tender

Townscape
The visual appearance and form of a town or city

Trust
A charitable organisation usually made up of a combination of organisations that exists for providing social benefits

Un-incorporated company
A company that is not formed or maintained as a legal corporation

Vertical element
Vertical features usually on a building's façade or along a street

Vision statement
An outline or statement of aims for the future providing a useful guide for developing project, programme and community priorities

Vista
A distant view past a series of landmarks especially one seen through an opening such as between rows of buildings or trees

Written specifications
A detailed description or assessment in writing of requirements, dimensions, materials and characteristics of a proposed project.

Further reading

Akpeki, T. and Temkin, T., *Getting value from consultants*, NCVO, 2004

Barton, H. Grant, M. and Guise, R., *Shaping neighbourhoods: a guide for health, sustainability and vitality*, Abingdon: Spon Press, 2003 reprinted 2004

Benson, J. F. and Roe, M. H. (eds.), *Landscape and sustainability*, Spon Press, 2000

Benson, J. F. and Roe, M. H. (eds.), *Urban lifestyles: Spaces, places, people*, Balkerna, 2000

Burns, D. et al, *Making community participation meaningful: a handbook for development and assessment*, The Policy Press with Joseph Rowntree Foundation, 2004

Carmona, M., Heath, T., Oc, T. and Tiesdell, S., *Public places, urban spaces: the dimensions of urban design*, Architectural Press, 2003

Chanan, G., *Local community involvement: a handbook for good practice*, European Foundation for the improvement of living and working conditions, 1999

Gaventa, S., *New public spaces*, Mitchell Beazley, 2006

Heron, J., *The complete facilitator's handbook*, Kogan Page, 1999

Home Office, *Together: tackling anti-social behaviour*, Home Office , 2003

Jochum, V., Pratten, B., and Wilding, K., *Civil renewal and active citizenship: a guide to the debate*, NCVO, 2005

The Landscape Institute, *Appointing a chartered landscape architect, guidelines for best value*, The Landscape Institute, 2000

The Landscape Institute, *Engaging a landscape consultant, guidance for clients on fees*, The Landscape Institute, 2002

The Landscape Institute, *Guide to procedure for competitive tendering*, The Landscape Institute, 2003

The Landscape Institute, *The landscape consultant's appointment*, The Landscape Institute, revised 1998

Gallacher, Pauline, *Everyday spaces, the potential of neighbourhood space*, Thomas Telford Ltd, 2005

Randall, R. and Southgate, J., *Co-operative and community group dynamics*, Barefoot Books, 1980

Rowe, A. M. and Wales, A., *Changing estates: a facilitator's guide to making community environment projects work*, Groundwork Hackney, 1999

New Economics Foundation and UK Community Participation Network, *Participation works! 21 techniques of community participation for the 21st century*, New Economics Foundation, 1998

Office of the Deputy Prime Minister (ODPM), *New localism - citizen engagement, neighbourhoods and public services: evidence from local government*, ODPM, 2005

ODPM, *Cleaner safer greener communities*, ODPM, 2004

ODPM and Home Office, *Safer places: the planning system and crime prevention*, Thomas Telford Ltd, 2004

Respect Task Force, *Respect action plan, Respect Task Force*, 2006

Wates, N., *The community planning handbook: how people can shape their cities, towns and villages in any part of the world*, Earthscan, 2000.

7 Acknowledgements

This guide has been generously sponsored by the Big Lottery Fund.

Stakeholders consulted

Big Lottery Fund
Civic Trust
Communities and Local Government (CLG)
Countryside Agency
Groundwork UK
Heritage Lottery Fund
Landscape Institute
Parklife
Solent Centre for Architecture + Design

Grateful thanks to the Glass-House Community Led Design and Groundwork Manchester, Salford and Trafford for sharing material to set out a common structure and language for community spaces. Many thanks to Juliet Bidgood (NEAT) and Christina McDonagh (CABE Space enabler) for their case study research. Thanks also to the following people: Seth Bennett (Hyde Park Source), Paul Bramhill and Diana Jones (GreenSpace), Dianne Browning (Friends of Barnard Park), Simon Cole (Groundwork Wakefield), Derek Fairchild and Jayne Vickers (Friends of St Neot Doorstep Green), Nicolas Falk (URBED), Gillian Fearnyough (The Architecture Centre), Helen Firminger (BOST), Pauline Gallacher, Johanna Gibbons (J&L Gibbons Landscape Architects), Dave Haygarth (Doorstep Greens Programme, Countryside Agency), Ben Hamilton-Baillie (Hamilton-Baillie Associates), Jacki Henderson (Groundwork Manchester, Salford and Trafford), John Hopkins (LDA Design), Pete Johnstone (Natural England), Dan Jones (civic Architects), Lynn Kinnear (Kinnear Landscape Architects), Steve McAdam (Fluid), Henriette Mortensen (Gehl Architects), Lisa Pontecorvo (Friends of Edward Square), Tom Putnam (Mapesbury Conservation Area Trust), Debra Samuel (Leeds Metropolitan University), Liz Smith (Southampton City Council), Steve Warren (Estell Warren), Adrian Wikeley (Land Use Consultants), Carole Woodward (Albion Residents' Association).